Getting A Clear Vision To Become A Millionaire

By

Dr. Kenton Edward Emmanuel Connor

TABLE OF CONTENT

COPYRIGHT

INTRODUCTION

They say there's nothing new under the sun all that has been will be, and all that will be has been, in short what goes around comes around. And so it is with thinking you see to become a millionaire you have to start with the correct thinking however this is where the biggest problems lie.

Let me explain, when we are born into this world kicking and screaming, naked and without inhibitions there are no boundaries placed upon us, no limitations on what we can and can't do. However as we grow older suddenly we are told, "oh no you can't do that" or "stop dreaming boy you could never do it" and where does this ambition suppression begin? In the one place you would expect creativity and ingenuity to thrive... School.

You see, at school they want you to excel but as a collective. Teachers discourage individualism they want you to conform fit in think small, be a team member. I want you to think hard about this one, did anything you learned at school teach you how to make serious money, or did it teach you how to get a job and be a slave for the rest of your existence?

I bet that if you even mentioned to anyone you wanted to become a millionaire, you were ridiculed and told to get real stop living in fantasy land. But here's the interesting thing most brilliant ideas start out as a dream that builds to a desire.

So to get rich and become a millionaire, you first need to have a dream or develop the habit of dreaming. And if your going to dream as Donald Trump says "You may as well dream big!" Next a dream is nothing without desire. Without desire the dream will remain but an illusion, then after desire you must have a concept a plan. You see desire alone will not get you to where you want to go, you have to plan how to get there.

After you've made your plan, you will need to implement your strategies by taking action, doing the things necessary to fulfill the big dream however tiny, every little step pulls you toward the big dream. Avoid distractions be

single-minded and steadfast with your ideals and beliefs. Believe it can happen and it will, do not be happy until you see the results you crave. This is the mind of a millionaire, There is a saying 'you are what you think about' what you focus on grows what you neglect dies.

So to sum up in order to become a millionaire one must develop the habit of correct thinking remove thoughts of negativity, and build a mind to succeed. Be strong of desire and conviction, only then can you become a millionaire.

BECOMING A MILLIONAIRE - A GOOD PLACE TO START

If your life is in a rut and you feel you are going nowhere especially on the subject of money then what you need do is take steps to get it started yourself. No-one is going to do it for you. There is nothing wrong in dreaming and fantasizing about what you want, so long as you take the required actions and steps to make it all manifest for you.

It is fine to make your vision board with pictures of all the things you want in life, it's fun and stimulating. Play all the money games you can think of, like pretending to spend $1000 every day and each day add another thousand so you get to spend more and remember to get the feeling of spending heaps of money so it becomes a 'normal' feeling for you. Whatever takes your fancy... it will all help you in your quest to becoming a millionaire. All these things give your intentions power and enhances your good 'feelings'. But that alone is not enough! You need to mobilize into action.

To get yourself started you need to take the step-by-step actions needed to help your 'wish list' materialize. Take note of any inspiration that comes to you that may help you start manifesting your desires. Be aware and notice opportunities that present themselves to you. After a while you will begin to see these opportunities as soon as they appear and take action instead of just dismissing it as an interesting thing that happened and then regret not taking action. If your aim is becoming a millionaire, then you will need to think like one.

Taking note of the happenings in your life is inspiring, positive and mind shifting. What your job is then, is to take up the challenge and figure out what steps you need to take to move forward to achieving your goal of becoming a millionaire. When you act quickly you get the opportunity to shine but when you delay, that opportunity will more than likely end up in the hands of the next willing person to take it and run.

Every person on this planet has a gift to give, never devalue yourself. The skills and talents

we all have can be of benefit to others. We all know something about a topic that others are interested in. Share what you know with others and reap the benefits that come from the act of sharing. Find your 'gap' in the marketplace - a need or desire that has been identified but not fulfilled. Use your skills to create a solution to the needs of others.

In this way you can be really creative and use your gifts, or co-ordinate the gifts of others to create services or products that have value to others. By doing this, you can create and generate an income for yourself and be well on the way to becoming a millionaire.

According to the 'Law of Income' - you are paid in direct relationship to the value you provide to others. If what you do can help others in some way to live a better life and succeed at something they wish to do, your value contribution will grow enormously. To receive value you need to give value - this is how the 'Law of Attraction' works. You get back what you put out - it's magnetic.

When you align your thoughts and actions with your life purpose, you have the power to live a more successful, abundant and happy life. When you start to consciously direct your thoughts to more positive outcomes, especially helping other people to succeed more in their lives, you will attract more of that into your experience as well. If you remember to use the three magic ingredients of Thought, Action and Providing Value - and become very good at it, you will have the ability to generate an income that will flow to you like a river. If you are not becoming a millionaire yet, then it could well be a problem within your own wealth blue-print. You need to actually create it in your mind first, only then can it become a reality.

By using the simple tools that you have inside yourself (your ability to care about what you think about and how you feel) you can actually start changing your life dramatically right away. Developing yourself as a person is an ongoing responsibility that you have to yourself. So don't wait, start developing your wealth muscles now - go out and find mentors who can help you on your path to success, whether it be marketing, real estate, share market or even just yourself as a person. You never stop learning.

HOW TO GET RICH GOD'S WAY FOR A PURPOSE

God does not have a problem with you being rich as long as He is first place in your life. In fact, He wants you rich because He needs you to help finance His endtime harvest of souls. And being your Heavenly Father, He wants you to dress the best, drive the best and live the best. He wants you on such a high financial plateau that the price of an item is never an issue. You're loaded. But slim chance this is going to happen if you're operating in the wrong system. Let's get you operating in the right system and bring you into your wealthy place.

There are two systems operating in this world. One is the world's system, it's failing. The other one is God's system, it never fails. The world's system says your job or the government is your source. If your job or the government doesn't offer you a rich man's income, your financially sunk. You will most likely be living on a budget from paycheck to paycheck. Your job and the government were never to be your source. God is to be your source.

"But my God shall supply all your need according to his riches in glory by Christ Jesus" (Philippians 4:19 KJV).

So what is your job or your monthly government paycheck? Your seed bin!

I'll explain. You see, God's system operates on a seedtime and harvest principle.

"While the earth remaineth, seedtime and harvest, and cold and heat, and summer and winter, and day and night shall not cease" (Genesis 8:22 KJV).

In a nutshell, here are 7 steps to bring you into your wealthy place:

1. To operate God's financial system you must be born into God's family by receiving Jesus Christ as your Lord and Savior.

2. You live to give. You become a sower, sowing financial seed where the Holy Spirit directs.

3. You must hear the voice of the Holy Spirit to receive His seed directed instructions. He will tell you how large a seed you are to sow and where to sow your seed. He doesn't want you sowing your seed in bad financial soil that will not produce a harvest.

4. Your financial seed you sow will probably come from your job or government income. Remember, your job or government income is your seed bin, not your harvest.

5. Like any wise farmer, you wait for your harvest. How does God multiply your financial seed sown to give you a harvest? He speaks to the hearts of people to give to you.

"Now he (God) that ministereth seed to the sower both minister bread for your food, and multiply your seed sown, and increase the fruits of your righteousness" (2 Corinthians 9:10 KJV).

Do you see how God uses your job or government income to provide you seed to sow, thus allowing Him to multiply your seed sown to give you a financial harvest. And of course, with each successive harvest comes larger and larger amounts of seed to sow, hence greater and greater harvests which bring you into your wealthy place.

6. So, how do you stay in faith between the time you sow your financial seed and the time your harvest manifests (comes in)? You daily thank, praise and worship God for giving you a financial harvest even though your harvest has not yet manifested. That's faith, rejoicing that your harvest has come in before you see it with your physical eyes. Faith says, "I've got it now." Doubt says, " I'll believe I have it when I see it with my physical eyes." Remember, none of this will work if you are not in faith. You must trust God to multiply your seed sown to give you financial harvests.

7. Enjoy your wealth. God wants you rich. Honor God in all you do as you seek Him and fulfill His desire for you to help finance His endtime harvest of souls.

Financial three step plans, money making formulas and sowing and reaping scriptures can all be well and good, but if you have a poverty stronghold lodged and hidden in your mind, you may never enter your earthly wealthy place. If you feel you might have a poverty mental stronghold keeping you from your wealthy place and you want to be set free, then click on "Free from a Poverty Mental Stronghold" below.

Jesus said, "If ye love me, keep my commandments." We are commanded by Him in Mark 16:15 to witness to the lost. Please don't be a disobedient Christian and lose your soul winner's crown awaiting you in heaven.

CHRISTIAN ONLINE BUSINESS

No inventory, no locked cash, no handling of returns, complains and credit adjustments! Although it sounds too good to be true, it VERY possible to find employment, start a business or find rewarding Christian income opportunities on the Internet. Learn how to keep your eyes and ears open all the time and resist the urge to jump onto the first bandwagon that drives up your lane and you should be perfectly fine.

Internet has made our world, which is divided by geography, race, personal beliefs, skin color, etc, into a borderless one. By making full use of some of the Christian job opportunities out there in the market today, you can reap handsome rewards.

The flexibility of time gives you time and focus on God and family There's no definite time for a work at home business or Christian income opportunity because you're your own boss. With flexible timing, you can choose to work whenever, whatever and however you want. There are tons of Christian-related income

opportunities out there in the market today. Although not all of them are credible or lucrative, most of them are legitimate ones.

With a PC or laptop, you can actually start a website selling Christian products. With your own internet website, there's no problem in diversifying or selling any other products or services...Internet offers you unlimited income opportunities and possibilities. And when you feel that you want to spend some time with God or your family, you can arrange your own time so that it suits your needs.

Running your own Christian Online Store can be easy as 1-2-3.Make a simple search on the internet about starting your own e-business and you will find ready made stores available at low cost. A word of caution if you're eager to grab all the Christian job opportunities that are thrown your way...be wary. As convenient as the Internet is, it has become close to impossible who is real and who isn't anymore. So, before you grab the employment of business opportunity, dig a little deeper beyond the surface by giving the website owner a call or sending the owner and email asking them about the Christian income opportunities that they are offering through their website.

No inventory, no locked cash, no handling of returns, complains and credit adjustments! Although it sounds too good to be true, it VERY possible to find employment, start a business or find rewarding Christian income opportunities on the Internet. Learn how to keep your eyes and ears open all the time and resist the urge to jump onto the first bandwagon that drives up your lane and you should be perfectly fine.

Its important to remember that nothing happens overnight. You should run in the other direction if any website owner or Christian income opportunity business owner tells you that by signing up with the affiliate program or becoming their reseller can make you a millionaire in three weeks! Happy searching!

HOW YOU CAN BE ONE OF GOD'S MILLIONAIRES

Because you are a Christian, you are targeted by God to become rich! Even so, in order to attain prosperity, you must keep in mind there is a clear distinction between income and wealth. Fact is, income and wealth are not the same thing. But, the good news is they are both under your direct control!

You see, if in spite of your Christian beliefs you stubbornly choose to live the kind of life-style that causes you to spend all of your income, and then both you and your children will suffer poverty, servitude and discouragement for the rest of your lives.

In short, if this is your own self imposed way of living, it can successfully oppose God's desire for you to be prosperous. This happens when you manage money your own way. After all, as you know, God gives us a free will that He will never take away. The end result is you and your children will always be under accumulators of wealth, in other words you will be poor.

Why? Because, with that kind of living pattern, you will never have any money left to accumulate in your bank account and to become your wealth. Why? Because wealth is what you accumulate with good management and by not spending.

What you can do, if you want to acquire wealth is listen to God's advice in Proverbs 22:4,6,7 and 800 other verses in the Bible, then make a high and holy resolve you will, henceforth, volunteer to live by His will for your life and thereby experience the joys and true wealth of the Christian life-style. When you do this, you'll find each day of your life will have its major emphasis on: prayer, hard work and perseverance so you can gain the benefits of carefully following a good money management plan.

The happy results of having money in the bank will make you smile because that kind of daily conduct will provide you with a gradual accumulation of wealth.

Surprisingly, you'll discover one benefit of wealth will be in the form of a big bank account. At the same time there is another important benefit, the training in money management you give your children when they follow your example later in their lives.

Let me say this another way, as your children watch you make those decisions for your family's good they will see what you do and in that way, gain a better understanding of the many benefits of the careful management of money. This kind of training can in turn, give them a more prosperous life-style in their futures.

Then they will gradually become large accumulators of wealth, just like their parents, who as everyone in the neighborhood knows are God's millionaires.

A MILLIONAIRE BLUEPRINT

Many of us like to dream to become a millionaire. It can be very simple and easy if you know how to master this 5 steps of millionaire blueprint.

Find a millionaire mentor

- A swimming coach can not teach you how to play basketball. Every successful people like Michael Jordan has their own coach. If you want to be a millionaire, the first step is to find a millionaire to be your mentor. They are the person who have been through the whole journey and know how to do it. Therefore, you can save lots of time and resources than do it on your own way. Please do some research to find one guru that suits you, invest in their courses and materials.

Start your own business

- Yes, start your own business no matter it is part time or full time. You may have many reasons or excuses for not starting your own business i.e. no time, no resources or not

enough capital etc. But the fact is, if you are working for somebody and getting a fixed pay, you are just being paid to be a working machine to help them to become a millionaire. Do you realize that 95% of the people in this world is working under the 5% business system, and the 95% of the people is not millionaire. So which Which category are you belong to? 5% or 95%?

Buy time with money

- Buy other people's time to run the business for you just like what your boss did. Do not do everything by yourself. Outsource some of the tasks i.e those time consuming and not at your expertise to some other people who does. So you can spend more time to strategize on how to multiply your income or expand your business. Trust me, this is the best way to do it because you only have 24 hours a day despite how intelligent you are. So, spend time on the more important thing.

Invest in real estate or stock market

- Majority of the millionaires are a sophisticated investor. They know how to play with the cash flow. They will not put all the eggs in one basket. However invest in property and stock market will need capital, one of my mentor taught me that do not to go into any investment until you have a stable income from your business. In other words passive income. Take this journey slowly and steadily. Do not rush into it.

Form a mastermind group

- Napoleon Hill, the best-selling author of "Think and Grow Rich" emphasized on how important of a mastermind group. You shall have many opportunities to meet new people when you join any wealth creation seminar. Remember to get their business card or a contact number. Arrange a monthly gathering if possible. Make them to be your buddy and adviser. These are the people who can help you, motivate you and encourage you along the the journey.

The list can go on and on but the key is to take action! The difference between a successful people and a failure is, a successful people take action and a failure only know how to find excuses for not doing anything. I believe you belong to the former who wish to be success. So, stop dreaming and take action now to hop onto the path to become a millionaire!

STEPS TO BECOME A MILLIONAIRE

Ever thought about you being a Millionaire? Ever thought about what it would take to become a Millionaire? Anyone ever shared with you how you can become a Millionaire? Interesting questions right?

I'm not sure about you, but no one ever sat me down and said, "Steve, this is what you need to do if you want to be a Millionaire." I've had to struggle through my life just like everyone else. The only difference is I've made many sacrifices in my life to learn from the correct people, I've read lots of books to expand my knowledge and value to the world and now I would like to take a few minutes to share with you 5 Steps to get you started so you can become a Millionaire.

1) See Yourself already As A Millionaire

Long before you can ever become a Millionaire, you need to start visualizing yourself as a Millionaire. Who will benefit from you being a Millionaire besides you?

How will you help people? What will you do with the money?

These are important ￼uestions. You can't just want to be a Millionaire and poof you are one. Sit down and create a vision that you can see in your own mind of you as a Millionaire. Think about is so much that you can see what you are wearing, what you drive for a car, who you are surrounded with and what house you are in.

The more details you can clearly see in your vision the more your mind will be able to help you start making it your reality.

2) Change Your Friends

This one may be really tough for a lot of you who are reading this. I don't want you to suddenly tell your existing friends they're not worthy of your time. But you do have to understand that you will stay at a success level of your closest friends.

If your closest friends make minimum wage, pick apart your dream and have none of their own, how likely do you think that you will become a Millionaire? If you start hanging around with people who want success, who strive for their goals in life and make a ton of money, you'll be forced to change. This will really help change your mindset and help you to start thinking like a Millionaire.

3) Stop Concerning Yourself With What People Think About You

Many people never take action because they are afraid that their closest friends and family will find out what they are doing. They are afraid they may even make fun of them. When they find out you actually have dreams and are working towards them, some of your friends may slam your dreams and be jealous.

Stop concerning yourself with what they think. You and only you know what you want, what you desire in life, that you want to be a Millionaire. Just because they are not willing to put in the time and effort to become a Millionaire, doesn't mean that you can't go for it.

You have to look out for yourself. Besides, when you become a Millionaire, think about how you'll be able to help inspire others to do the same as you did. How would that feel?

4) Believe In Yourself

OK, so you now have a vision for yourself of you being a Millionaire. You've reached out to some new friends who are more successful than you and never give up on their goals. You have stopped concerning yourself with what others think. Now, you need to start believing in yourself.

One good way to start believing in yourself is to use affirmations. Think about the steps you need to go through to become a Millionaire. Write down the first few that will be easiest to accomplish on a piece of paper. Then re-write them every night before you go to bed and again when you first wake up. This is when your brain will best use the information. Write them as a ?uestion and form the ?uestion as you have already accomplished them.

This will start training your sub-conscious that you already have accomplished these affirmations and your mind will help you start making them your reality.

The sooner you believe you can really become a Millionaire, the sooner it will really happen. The only person who can make you a Millionaire is you. Start believing in yourself today!!!

5) Take Massive Action

Once you have your vision of you becoming a Millionaire, it's time to take Massive Action. It's not time to tip toe around and think about how to become a Millionaire. It's time to get started and really go for it.

Remember though, this will not happen overnight. This is a marathon, not a sprint. So please pace yourself. Do you think Tiger Woods became the world's best golfer by hitting 1,000,000 balls in a month. No! He hits thousands of balls every single week. He took massive action every single day to get to where he wanted to be. You can do the same.

www.ingramcontent.com/pod-product-compliance
Lightning Source LLC
Chambersburg PA
CBHW031508210526
45463CB00003B/1128